Three Streets Productions presents

FIJI LAND

BY NICK GILL

8 - 11 January 2014, Burton Taylor Studio, Oxford

15 January - 8 February 2014,
Southwark Playhouse, London

T0321550

CAST
in alphabetical order

Grainer	Jake Ferretti
Tanc	Stephen Bisland
Wolstead	Matthew Trevannion

CREATIVE

Director	Alice Malin
Designer	Ruth Hall
Lighting Designer	Tom Wickens
Associate Lighting Designer	Matthew Swithinbank
Sound Designer	Max Pappenheim
Stage Manager	Louise Rouse
Fight Director	Robin Colyer
Producers	Ashleigh Wheeler
	Vicki Grace

This production is supported by Arts Council England and Magdalen College School, Oxford.

The performance lasts approximately one hour and ten minutes without an interval. We regret that there is no admittance or re-admittance to the auditorium whilst the performance is in progress.

Jake Ferretti
Grainer

Jake was recently part of the ensemble for the original West End cast of *The Curious Incident of the Dog in the Night-Time.* Other theatre credits include *The Kitchen* (National Theatre), *Sherlock Holmes* (Erasmus Theatre), *The Wind Doesn't Sing*, *Graceland* (Old Vic New Voices), *Enjoy* (Gielgud Theatre and UK Tour), *Pygmalion* (Old Vic Theatre), *Romeo and Juliet* (Teatro di Stabile, Verona), and *Cloud Nine* (Edinburgh Festival).

Stephen Bisland
Tanc

Stephen trained at the Royal Welsh College of Music and Drama. Theatre credits include *The Hairy Ape* (Southwark Playhouse), and *The Man Who Had All the Luck* (Mull Theatre). Television credits include *Doctors* and *Waterloo Road*.

Matthew Trevannion
Wolstead

Recent theatre credits include *Beautiful Burnout* (Frantic Assembly/ National Theatre of Scotland), *Little Dogs* (Frantic Assembly/National Theatre of Scotland), *Dr Dee* (ENO), *The Sea Plays* (Old Vic Tunnels), *Hamlet* (Young Vic), and *Love Steals Us from Loneliness* (National Theatre Wales). Matthew is also an award nominated playwright whose debut play *Bruised* was first performed at the Clwyd Theatr Cymru and has since been translated into several languages. He is currently under commission to write new work for both the National Theatre Wales and Sherman Cymru.

Nick Gill
Playwright
Nick Gill is a playwright, composer and musician. Writing includes *Sand* (Royal Court, dir. Vicky Featherstone) and *Mirror Teeth* (Finborough, dir. Kate Wasserberg [production nominated for 4 Off West End Awards]). As one of The Apathists, several shorts were staged at Theatre503 and various venues 2006-2008, directed by Polly Findlay, Lyndsey Turner and Duncan Macmillan, among others. Music includes *One million* (Greenwich & Docklands International Festival), *Schwarze spiegel* (Studio Hrdinů, Czech Republic), *Gilbert is dead*, (Hoxton Hall), *Thrown* (Royal Court), *Knock Out* (Deutschlandradio Kultur) and *Pandora's Box* (BFI Southbank).

Alice Malin
Director
Recent credits include *Freefall: A Double Bill* (New Wimbledon Studio), *The Ones Who Kill Shooting Stars* (White Bear Theatre), *XX, Diggers, Citizenship* (Theatre503), *Fox* (Descent/Southwark Playhouse), *In The Garage* (Little Pieces of Gold at Southwark Playhouse), *Baggage* (Soho Theatre), *Loot* (Cockpit Theatre), *Seven* (George Tavern), and *The Bird Trap* (Lost Theatre). Assistant director credits include *Dancing at Lughnasa* (Northampton Theatre Royal), *Where the Mangrove Grows* (Theatre503), *Roots, As You Like It* (Clwyd Theatr Cymru).

Ruth Hall
Designer
Recent credits include *Pridd* (Theatre Genedlaethol Cymru), *Noah* (Theatre on the Fly, Chichester Festival Theatre), *Roots*, costumes for *Glengarry Glen Ross*, *Educating Rita*, *Sky Hawk*, *Jac and the Falling Apples* and *Humbug!* (all Clwyd Theatr Cymru), *The Ones Who Kill Shooting Stars* (White Bear Theatre), *Riot* (The North Wall), *The Road To Mecca* (Arcola), *Patagonia – The Long Journey* (National Youth Theatre of Wales), *Kindertransport* (Aberystwyth Arts Centre), *Captain Oates' Left Sock*, *Too Good To Be True*, and *The Killing of Mr Toad* (all Finborough Theatre), *The Phoenix and the Turtle* (Royal Shakespeare Company Complete Works Festival).

Tom Wickens
Lighting Designer
Recent credits include *Paco Peña – Quimeras* (Sadler's Wells & Tour), *The Ones Who Kill Shooting Stars* (White Bear), *Billy the Kid* (Southwark Playhouse), *In Lambeth* (Stephen Joseph Theatre), *The Scandalous Case of Dr Jekyll and Mr Hyde* (Edinburgh and London). Relights include *Top Girls* (Out of Joint), *Paco Peña – Flamenco Sin Fronteras* (UK and international tours), *Communicating Doors* (Stephen Joseph Theatre) and *Ballet Black* (Orpheus UK tour). Associate credits include *The Colored Museum* (Talawa), *Shiverman* (Theatre503), *Red Light Winter* (Theatre Royal Bath). Tom is currently Deputy Chief Electrician at the Donmar Warehouse.

Matthew Swithinbank
Associate Lighting Designer
Matthew Swithinbank is a lighting designer and technician from Luxembourg with an interest in projection and video. He trained at Mountview Academy of Theatre Arts on the Theatre

Production Arts course. Credits include lighting designs for *Jane Eyre* at the Abbaye Neumunster in Luxembourg City, *The Devil His Due* at the Festival of European Anglophone Theatre Societies in Geneva, *Palimpsest One* at Upstairs at the Gatehouse, *Dead Funny* and *Our Walk Through The World* at the Old Red Lion, *The Chrysalids* at the Sir John Cass Foundation School, and AV design for *Midas* at the Karamel Club and St James Theatre.

Max Pappenheim
Sound Designer
Sound Design and Composition includes *Our Ajax* (Southwark Playhouse), *Mrs Lowry and Son* (Trafalgar Studios), *CommonWealth* (Almeida Theatre), *Black Jesus*, *Summer Day's Dream*, *The Hospital at the Time of the Revolution*, *Somersaults*, *The Soft of Her Palm*, *The Fear of Breathing* (Finborough Theatre), *Being Tommy Cooper* (UK Tour), *Irma Vep*, *Borderland*, *Kafka v Kafka* (Brockley Jack Studio Theatre), *Four Corners One Heart* (Theatre503), *Freefall: A Double Bill* (New Wimbledon Theatre Studio), *The Ones Who Kill Shooting Stars* (White Bear Theatre) and *Below the Belt* (Pleasance, Edinburgh). Associate credits include *The Island* (Young Vic).

Louise Rouse
Stage Manager
Trained at the Royal Welsh College of Music and Drama. Theatre includes *Blinda* (Volcano Theatre Company, Swansea), *Whispers on the Waves* (Weston Studio, Wales Millenium Centre, Cardiff), *Orpheus In The Underworld* (Coal Exchange, Cardiff), *The Girl With The Iron Claws* (Arcola Theatre, London), *Dandelion* (Welsh Tour), *Stories of the Streetz* (St David's Hall, Cardiff).

Robin Colyer
Fight Director
As a qualified stage combat teacher under the British Academy of Dramatic Combat (BADC) and the Academy of Performance Combat (APC), Robin has taught for a number of leading leading drama schools, including Guildford School of Acting, Royal Welsh College of Music and Drama, Oxford School of Drama and East 15. In addition to his work as an independent fight director, Robin is an Artist in Residence at Oxford Playhouse in his role as Artistic Director for emerging theatre company, Flintlock Theatre.

Ashleigh Wheeler
Producer
Ashleigh is Resident Producer at Oxford Playhouse/Magdalen College School 2013-14. She is also Participation Producer for Up in Arms theatre company, whose credits include *Visitors* (Arcola Theatre and UK tour) and *Fear of Music* (UK tour).

Vicki Grace
Producer
Vicki is co-founder and producer for Three Streets Productions whose credits include *Freefall: A Double Bill of World Premieres* (New Wimbledon Studio) and *The Ones Who Kill Shooting Stars* (White Bear Theatre). She has worked extensively in arts development for organisations including Shakespeare's Globe and The Guildhall School of Music & Drama.

Production Acknowledgements

Production Image and Poster Design
Rebecca Pitt
www.rebeccapitt.co.uk
Production Photography
Dan Smyth
www.dansmythphotography.com

Funders

Magdalen College School, Oxford

Thanks to
Magdalen College School, Oxford Playhouse,
Southwark Playhouse, Michelle Walker, Nick Quinn,
Steve Heywood, Rob Bristow, Philippa Baines.

About Three Streets Productions

Three Streets Productions is a platform for bold work by exciting new playwrights. Recent work includes *Freefall: A Double Bill of World Premieres*, comprised of two new plays, *Lacuna* by Matthew Bulgo and *The Bear, The Owl and The Angel* by Becky Prestwich, which ran at the New Wimbledon Studio from 10 - 13 July 2013; *The Ones Who Kill Shooting Stars* by Stewart Parker Award-winning playwright Conall Quinn at the White Bear Theatre from 2 – 21 October 2012; and *The Bird Trap* by Hennessey Literary Award nominee Darren Donohue at the Lost Theatre in May 2012. Three Streets Productions have also produced various short plays across London and run regular readings and script development workshops for new plays.

www.threestreetsproductions.co.uk

Follow Us Online
@Three_Streets
www.facebook.com/ThreeStreetsProductions

'Southwark Playhouse's brand is as quirky as it is classy'
The Stage

Southwark Playhouse is all about telling stories and inspiring the next generation of storytellers and theatre makers. It aims to facilitate the work of new and emerging theatre practitioners from early in their creative lives to the start of their professional careers.

Through our schools work we aim to introduce local people at a young age to the possibilities of great drama and the benefits of using theatre skills to facilitate learning. Each year we engage with over 5,000 school pupils through free schools performances and long-term in school curriculum support.

Through our Young Company (YoCo), a youth-led theatre company for local people between the ages of 11-25, we aim to introduce young people to the many and varied disciplines of running a semi-professional theatre company. YoCo provides a training ground to build confidence and inspire young people towards a career in the arts.

Our theatre programme aims to facilitate and showcase the work of some of the UK's best up and coming talent with a focus on reinterpreting classic plays and contemporary plays of note. Our two atmospheric theatre spaces enable us to offer theatre artists and companies the opportunity to present their first fully realised productions. Over the past 20 years we have produced and presented early productions by many aspiring theatre practitioners many of whom are now enjoying flourishing careers.

What People Say...

'An astounding venue' **The Guardian**

'High-achieving, life-giving spirit'
Fiona Mountford, Evening Standard

'...the revitalised Southwark Playhouse'
Lyn Gardner, The Guardian

'Southwark Playhouse churn out arresting productions
at a rate of knots' **Time Out**

'I love that venue so much. It is, without doubt, one of the
most exciting theatre venues in London.'
Philip Ridley, Playwright

For more information about our forthcoming season and to book tickets visit **www.southwarkplayhouse.co.uk**. You can also support us online by joining our Facebook and Twitter pages.

OP

OXFORD PLAYHOUSE

Oxford Playhouse and its Burton Taylor Studio present and produce a wide range of live performance. The programme includes the best of British and international drama, family shows, contemporary dance and music, student and amateur shows, comedy, lectures and poetry. The Playhouse also creates live performance in Oxford. It produces and tours its own shows, has Shared Experience as its resident company, supports emerging artists with the Evolve: Artists in Residence programme, and presents Playhouse Plays Out – an ongoing series of off-site events, taking surprising theatre to unexpected places across the county.

The Learning team works with over 14,000 people each year through post-show discussions, workshops, work experience, three resident young people's theatre companies and holiday schemes.

Recent producing credits for Oxford Playhouse include: *Sancho* written and directed by Paterson Joseph; *The Story of the Four Minute Mile*, performed on the Iffley Road running track; *Lionboy*, a co-production with Complicite; Charles Dickens' *Curiosity Shop*, a co-production with Theatre Alibi, and *The Oxford Poetry Walk*, a co-production with Live Canon. In 2013 we supported our resident company Shared Experience with their production *Bracken Moor* at the Tricycle Theatre and supported Kenneth Emson's *England Street* in our BT studio, produced by Polly Ingham Productions and MCS Drama. In 2014 Oxford Playhouse will be creating a season of new productions celebrating Oxford as a home of *Radical Thinking*, working with artists including Chris Goode, Polly Teale, Molly Naylor and Nick Walker.

www.oxfordplayhouse.com

FIJI LAND

.

Nick Gill

FIJI LAND

OBERON BOOKS
LONDON

WWW.OBERONBOOKS.COM

First published in 2014 by Oberon Books Ltd
521 Caledonian Road, London N7 9RH
Tel: +44 (0) 20 7607 3637 / Fax: +44 (0) 20 7607 3629
e-mail: info@oberonbooks.com
www.oberonbooks.com

A catalogue record for this book is available from the British Library.

PB ISBN: 978-1-78319-090-4
E ISBN: 978-1-78319-589-3

Typeset in Joanna MT by Oberon Books Ltd.

Cover design by Rebecca Pitt
www.rebeccapitt.co.uk

Printed, bound and converted
by CPI Group (UK) Ltd, Croydon, CR0 4YY.

Visit www.oberonbooks.com to read more about all our books and to
buy them. You will also find features, author interviews and news of
any author events, and you can sign up for e-newsletters so that you're
always first to hear about our new releases.

To all who have supported and inspired with their seemingly-endless generosity — Mike Bartlett, Caryl Churchill, Duncan Macmillan, Morgan Lloyd Malcolm, Simon Stephens, Simon Vinnicombe, Rachel Wagstaff, and my wonderful parents — thank you.

I would like humbly to dedicate this play to those throughout the world whose suffering can't be done justice by a simple piece of fiction.

And to Ve, whom I love like Brâncuși loved marble.

n

Characters

GRAINER

TANC

WOLSTEAD

A containment unit.
Neon lights.
Rows and rows of flowering plants stand in pots.

Three guards –
Grainer
Tanc
Wolstead

A line of empty dialogue indicates an active silence.

This part of the prison was in an open space and consisted of five sectors, surrounded by walls and barb wires and was called 'Fiji Land'. Each sector had five tents and surrounded by barb wires. When I was removed from the truck, the soldiers marked my forehead with the words 'Big Fish' in red. All the detainees in this camp are considered 'Big Fish'.

Ali Shalal , 7th February 2007

a)

A containment unit, in a state of disarray — smashed plant pots, piles of soil.

Time passes.

GRAINER is asleep.
WOLSTEAD is watching him.

Time passes.

G   jesus
W   hello
G   what the fucking
      jesus
      the fuck are you doing?
W   I'm watching you sleep
G   what
      what, you're
      you're watching me sleep?
W   you do this thing with your mouth sometimes
      like this:
      grabblababarg
      what's that all about?
G   what?
W   that thing
      grabblababarg
      what's going on with that?
G   I don't
      who the fuck are you?
W   you don't even know you're doing it
      do you?
G   doing the
      what?
W   did you do all this?
      bit of a state, isn't it?

G   what?

no, course not, you

ok

who are you?

what you doing here?

serious, now

what the fuck you doing,

watching people sleep, eh?

W   don't get much chance

don't see folks asleep that often

not when they're supposed to be working

bit of a rarity, that

G

look

alright

yeah, you got me, but look

it's not like anything happened, is it?

W   didn't it?

how do you know?

only takes one little slip to let something by, doesn't it?

you might wake up and find someone's been watching you

for half an hour

someone who could have done something terrible

could have done something to you, even

G

W   I didn't

G   good

W   certainly is

G

fucking hell, nothing happened

W   calm calm calm

nothing to fluster thy tiny mind with

alright?

G

 so

 fuck, ok

 so you're the other guy

W I'm the first guy

 you're the other guy

G

W well, no

 first guy's on his way

 you're still the other guy

G fucking hell

 so

 who are you, then?

W no names

G

W for the best

G uh huh

 going to make things a bit difficult, isn't it?

W what 'things'?

G

W it'll work out alright, you know

 I think you might be one of those people who worry too

 much

Enter TANC.

T good

 hello

 alright

 first – clean up

G who are you?

T
    I'm the first guy
W   told you
T   go on
    both of you
    you can listen while you clear this place up

    first, clean up
    good
    second, welcome all
    this is the place

    this is where it all goes on

    right?
    the job's easy
    keep watch
    stay alert
    don't fuck around
    orders come in, you follow them
    two on, one off
    questions
G   uh
    you in charge?
T   sure
G   what do we call you?
T   no names
    easiest that way
G   course
    ok
    what if there's a problem?
T   deal with it
G   uh huh
    and if we're running low on big-man bullshit?

T

    do your fucking job

    alright?

    you knew what you were getting into

    they might well have told you you were going to be a golden

    crusader

    blazing through the fucking desert darkness

    but that, as you will soon come to realise

    is not what we are here for

    so do your fucking job

    yes, I'm in charge

    no, you might not know what you're doing

    but you're being paid well

    so don't fuck around

    follow your orders

    get that lot cleaned up

    do your time

Alarm sounds.

T   water them

G

T   water

    them

G   right

T

    you're not saying much

W

    there much to say?

T

    good

b)

G   no, sure
     right
     but they don't
     I mean
     them?
T   's what we're here for
G   right
T   you knew what you were getting into
G

     yeah, but

T   but?
G   's not what

     I expected

     that's all
T   golden crusader, eh?
     orders
G   sorry?
T   orders come in
     we follow them
     and we watch them
     simple
G   company man

     dangerous way to think, though

     dangerous indeed

     always got to question, haven't you?

     get led all sorts of places otherwise

14

don't you?

T

    I'm going say it again, alright?

    follow your orders

    do what you're told

    do it proper

G

    yeah?

    wasn't that the Nazis' excuse?

T   jesus

    do your job

    they're not dangerous

    don't worry about it

G   right

    right

Time passes.

G   you don't wonder what's going on?

T   get paid the same

G   sure

    but, still

    you don't want to know about

    you know

    ?

T   I don't want to get into a discussion about this

    alright?

G   can't just stick your head in the sand, though, can you?

T   didn't say that

G   fighting the good fight

T   jesus

G   that what we're doing, is it?

T

    you should talk less

G   why, is that
       is that a threat?

T

G

T   it's tiring

G
       you fed them?

T   not yet
       when the alarm goes

G

T

G   you smoke?

T   no

G   pity

T   you?

G   no
       something to do though

T

G

T   how long you been here?

G   here?
       dunno
       not long

T   ah
       right

G   what?

T   nothing

G   come on
       what?

T   just
       heh
       bored already

G   got an active mind

T   course you do

G   you know, if you don't want to think about any of this stuff,
you are in the wrong fucking place, my friend
you know?
that's why I
alright, look, I asked to come over here, yeah
see some of the stuff that's going on
get involved, you know?
yeah, ok, I didn't buy it all, but still, yeah
bit of the crusader shit
but make a fucking difference, right?
fight the good fight

there's all sorts of shit's going on that you just don't hear
about

so, yeah
this isn't the time to look away

T   first up
I am not your friend.

second
there's nothing to find out

G   fuck's sake

T   there's nothing
there is nothing

look around
look around you
go on

there's nothing here
there's just

bureaucracy at work

 look, you want something to do?

Alarm sounds.

T   feed them
G

GRAINER sprays the plants.

T   not the last row
G   what?
T   not the last row

 orders
G
 you're kidding me
T
G

GRAINER continues watering.

G   so this is it

 this is what we do, is it?

 this is
 this
 is making a difference, is it?

 and you don't wonder about any of it?
T   just
 ugh
 mind your own business
 don't get squeamish
G   squeamish?
 ha

orders
orders
orders

so how long've you been here?
T   I have to go out

keep watch

pack of cards there
couple of skin mags

the other guy'll be in later
G   thought I was the other guy
T

c)

Time passes.

W you could have put the eight on the nine

G what?

W the eight

on the nine

if you'd done that, you could have opened up that sixth row,
and then everything might have turned around

oh, no

wouldn't have mattered anyway

G jesus

think I preferred the other guy

W

what other guy?

G that guy you took over from

the other guy

W

what are you talking about?

G fuck's sake

the first guy, then

alright?

W you alright?

there's only two of us

that's how it works

one on, one off

G what?

no, no, fuck off

he was here

just here, earlier on

wasn't

W

    no, I'm just fucking around

    got to pass the time somehow

G   jesus

W   hey

    come over here, will you?

G   what?

    why?

W   I need to take a picture

G   what?

W   a photo

    I need to take a photograph

G   of me?

W   yes of you

G   why?

W   uh

    full of questions, aren't you?

    I need to take a photo so I can send it to my loving mum and dad back home

    ok?

G

    you're serious

W   yeah, course

    sort of postcard

G   no paper?

W   oh ho ho

    better

    got a budget, haven't we?

    billions and billions of pounds sitting in big camouflaged coffers

    day they make gold-plated film, I'm getting a crate of them

G   don't they notice?

W   notice what?

G   spending all their money on film

W

    are you

    ?

    aw, you poor sweet lamb

    you're serious, aren't you?

G   what?

W   poor little newbie

G   fuck off

    newbie

    fuck off with that

    how long you been here?

    hmm?

    whole place is being watched, right?

    isn't it?

    they're gonna notice

W   heh

    look

    I don't have the time to explain the intricacies of quasi-military economics, alright?

G   fuck off, would you?

    patronising cunt

W   temper

    look, it's fine

    don't lose any sleep for me, ok?

    they're not going to notice

    it's fine

    shush thy tiny mind

    come on

    standing in front of them, please

G   in front of them?

W   to give a

    what's it called?

    a flavour of the place

         come on
         say hello to mister and missus

WOLSTEAD takes a photo.

W   et voilà
         here
         hold that for a sec

         don't bother
         it's a myth
G   what?
W   shaking them
         doesn't make it work quicker
G
W   look, shake it if you want
         do a little dance
         it'll take its own sweet time whatever
G   it works
         I've seen it
W   if it makes you happy, you go for it
         shake away
         sometimes stuff just
         happens without you

         you know?
G   thought they stopped making these
W   they did
         for a while, anyway
         company bought up boxes and boxes of them
G   what they want film for?
         thought it was all digital now
W   evidence
G   what?
W   e

vi

dence

take one of them, that's all there is

little bit of paper

digital stuff, well

someone slips, gets nervous, sends an email, suddenly the thing's fucking everywhere

paper, film

keeps it in the room

it goes missing, you know what you're looking for

it's not going far

G   you're posting them

W

every system has flaws

Alarm sounds.

G

W

G   not my job now

three past

your go

W

G   not the last

W   not the last row, yeah

I know

WOLSTEAD waters the plants.

W   has it come out yet?

G   nope

W   maybe you're not shaking it hard enough

G   fuck off

there we go

god

      I look awful

W   that's what you look like

G   not it's not

W   camera doesn't lie

G   fucking does

      lies all the time

      look at that

W   what?

G   that

      that is not what I look like

W   yes it is

      that's you

G   the fuck do you know

      fucking ten quid camera

      what you writing?

W   told you

      postcard

G   what

      it's really for your mum and dad?

W   yep

      'dear mum'

      'this is my new colleague'

      'he is already getting on my fucking tits'

      'send biscuits'

      'love'

      'your son'

G   that's funny

      you're really funny

W   I try

      you know

      someone finds out you've been sleeping on watch

      you could be in a lot of trouble

G   heh

what, here?

W   what about here?

not exactly gathered to the bosom of the law here, are we?

what,

you think they'd just send you home, or something?

G

and how exactly would they find out?

W   I don't know

people find out things all sorts of ways

don't they?

photos, for example

G

you said you didn't do anything

W

I did

didn't I?

G

I'm going out

W   where to?

there's nothing out there

can you post that on the way?

G

sure

W   grabblababarg

G

d)

G

    that guy

T   yes

G   is he

    you know

    alright?

T

    depends what you mean

G   I mean

    is he fucking mental?

T   probably

G

    five on the six

    and where did he get that fucking camera from?

T   don't know

    might've been here already

    might've been left

G   by who?

T

    last bloke

G

    what last bloke?

    hmm?

T

    bloke who was here before him

    before you

G   bit weird

    isn't it?

T   I'm not his fucking keeper

G

    alright
    he taken any
    any pictures of you?

T   he's taken pictures of everything

G

    does he really send them to his mum and dad?

T   you sent one, didn't you?

G   yeah, but there's no stamp on it or anything

T   central sorting office
    they pick everything up
    gets franked when it comes through

G   typical
    centralised everything

T

G   that's the thing, isn't it?
    yeah
    centralised power like that
    taking care of what we need
    sending out orders
    need to know basis
    all that
    so no one like us
    out here
    doing the work
    we don't have any responsibility, do we?

    nothing we do's our fault

    just doing what we're told

T

G   so what does he mean
'quasi-military economics'?

T

G   sorry, am I bothering you?
not like there's anything else to do

T

concentrating

G   yeah
one pack of cards in the room
two of us sat here
and you're playing fucking solitaire

T

G

just making conversation

so what do you think about his economics thing?

T   don't know

G

jack on the queen
jesus
haven't you played this fucking game before?

T

G   I dunno
don't think I can trust him

T

G   you don't get that?
he's

I dunno
he's weird
does weird stuff
says weird stuff

T

G   made these kind of

well

sort of threats

I don't think he's one of us

you know?

not a team player

T

who said it was a team?

besides

he's good at his job

doesn't ask questions

G

alright

maybe

but he's a thief

T   is he, now?

G   he said as much

seemed proud of it, too

about how he'd never get caught

T   well, then

G   what

you don't think it matters?

T   look –

no one cares

right?

no one cares what we do

as long as we're here, doing what we're told

no one cares

G   oh come on

T   only about six people even fucking know we're here

let alone what we're doing

we do what we're supposed to

and the world's a better place
right?
no one needs to know we're here
or what we're doing with these things
what happens in the sheds
what we put in the ovens
or what we order in from stores
someone pinching a bit of film's a fair price for world peace

don't you think?

G   sure

nine on the ten

so
I guess people must fall asleep on watch all the time
T   mmm
G

you ever fallen asleep?
on watch?
T

no
why?
G   no reason

anyway
just saying
we should keep an eye on him
T

Alarm sounds.

G   I'll do it

not the last row
I know

e)

W   alright, so
       your basic military-industrial complex

       sitting comfortably?

G

W   heh
       so
       in the beginning, there were a couple of guys who got into a
       fight
       right?

G   fuck's sake

W   and eventually this fight turned ugly
       so each of these guys got all their mates involved
       to help them beat up the other guys
       and, of course, some of the people turned out to be pretty
       good at fighting
       some of them, not so much
       but the good ones, now
       they were the sort who could get the job fucking done
       you know?
       so those were the ones you had to keep happy

       the ones who were rubbish, didn't need them
       they could fuck off back home and grow stuff

       you want the good ones
       the ones who know what they're doing
       they're the ones you need to keep happy
       'cos they're the ones holding the sharp sticks in the night

       and thus, little one, was The Military born

       so, fast forward a couple of thousand years

not that much's changed
still need to keep these guys happy, don't we?
so the army needs stuff
lots of stuff –
guns, tanks, uniforms, diodes, bullets, wart cream, transistors,
tampons, copy paper, ink cartridges, you name it –
and, to even be considered by your military purchasers, every
single thing has to be made to precise specifications, with no
hidden features, no bugs, high reliability and for an affordable
cost

these days, of course, that includes your soldiers
outsourced personnel, see?

anyway, if you're a manufacturer
you win an army contract and you are quids in, round to the
front of the queue and quids in once again, not to mention
the prestige back home for your domestic commercial market

so there's a lot of competition among these companies for
who gets to supply them, or us, with these things

I don't know
computers, say

let's say there's a war going well, lots of insurgents are
surrendering
say the military wants a way of keeping track of them
they put out a call for tenders, tenders come in, blah blah blah
say, I don't know, IBM gets it

just an example
they've got form, though
remember them tattoos in Belsen?
Auschwitz?

who do you think came up with that?
good system, too
worked well

two on the three

now
to win this contract, the head of IBM has cut his profits back
so far that he doesn't make that much on a single laptop
so, the only way he can continue to keep his Tuscan villa
with the gorgeous portico is if the army continues to buy his
company's products in huge quantities for a long period of
time

a very long fucking period of time

ok
so there's your industrial side
over to the military now –

are you cold?
feels cold in here

now
General Hamer
or whoever you want
now, he likes his job
he's been in combat before
not too much, because he went to officer school and it's a lot
of money to train someone like that
lot of money to lose if he gets hit in the head out on some
scouting job
but he's seen enough to know he doesn't like it
so these days, General Hamer likes being sat behind his desk,
with his special uniform and his shiny sword

now for his job to be secure, his budget needs to be secure
and the best way to prove to the purse holders that the budget
is absolutely necessary
is to spend it
spend every last fucking penny

how many cars have we got sitting out there?
you ever seen them move?
hmm?

everyone's got a laptop
there's wifi fucking everywhere
you reckon it's strategically vital that everyone out there can
look at kittens and tits twenty-four-seven?
think we really need all them plasma TVs?
armour-plated flash drives?

both sides win
IBM and General Hamer, they prop each other up
their jobs, their incomes, their villas, they're all safe
back home, the country feels safe with a well-funded military
and wherever they are, your personnel have little comforts to
make their lives that shade easier

so, in conclusion, little one –
they couldn't give even half a fuck

no one cares about a couple of boxes of film
even if they did, what are they going to do?
I'm keeping IBM rich
the military well-funded
country safe

I'm a fucking hero

WOLSTEAD takes a photo.

> my advice to you –
> order a Playstation
> and keep your mouth shut

f)

TANC is cutting tiny slivers from some plants.

G

    ha

    right

    listen

    you listening?

T

G   'So we have a choice: do we maintain properly funded, properly governed intelligence and security services, which will gather intelligence on these people, using all of the modern techniques to make sure that we can get ahead of them and stop them, or do we stop doing that?'

    too fucking right, mate

    what you doing?

T

    orders

G   what

    new ones?

    didn't tell me about anything like that

T   they're not for you

    it's just

    some stuff

G   what sort of stuff?

T

    doesn't matter

G   right

    sort of experiment

    is it?

T   it's all legitimate

G   right

T   orders

G   yeah, alright

     jesus I'm hot

     aren't you hot?

T   no

G   must be used to it, I guess

T   used to it?

G

     yeah

     you know

     how long you been out here?

T

     don't know

     a while

G   yeah

     see?

     acclimatised

     that's it

T   acclimatised

G   yeah

     don't they get on your fucking nerves?

T   what?

G   them

     they just sit there

     expecting to get looked after

T

G   bit weird

     looking after these things

T   there's a reason

G   yeah

there's always a fucking reason
just depends on whether we're allowed to know it
right?

T

G   ooh
you're not looking so good, are you?
not like your little friends
don't like not having any water, do you?
maybe that'll teach you a fucking lesson

T   eh?
G   what?
T
G   what?

Alarm sounds.

G   ah
and now everyone gets to drink

think I might join you
except you
and you
and you
all of you
you little fuckers get nothing
hope you fucking suffer

why them?
T
don't know
G   must be some reason

why it's them, I mean
jesus

how are you not hot?
I'm fucking roasting

you mind if I take this off?
T   go for it
G

that's better
don't know how you stand it
T

stand what?
G   the fucking heat
what else?
T

G
T   doesn't feel hot to me

the last two
there
G   these ones?
T   yeah
take them out to the ovens
G
T

the ovens
out the front
G

right
T   there's someone out there already
just hand them over to him
get him to sign this
G

right

g)

W   so
       what's he been saying to you?
G
W   hmm?
G
W   what's he been talking about?
G   nothing
W   right

       he's not told you
       you know
       what's going on, then?
G   what's going on?
       no
       doesn't talk about anything much
W   course he doesn't
       that's his trick
G   what?
W   stays aloof, doesn't he?
       makes sure he's not down to our level
       doesn't want to get involved, see?
       means he can keep us in the dark
G

       right
W   you put in that order yet?
G   not yet
W   you should
       got to have some entertainment
       haven't you?

       get that new Xbox or something
       they're good, they are
G   mmm

```
        you
        you know anything about these ovens?
W       what?

        what ovens?
G       out the front
        the ovens
W       haven't seen any ovens
G       had to take a couple of them out there yesterday
W       couple of them?
G       yep
W

        right

        probably best not to think about it
        sure it's nothing
G       yeah
W       wouldn't worry about it
G

        so
        you know what else is out there?
W       been through this
        there's nothing out there
G       sure
        but there's more
        you know
        more places like this, right?

        what's in them?
        more of them?
W       maybe
G       something else?
W       dunno
```

      maybe

G   there's a lot of units out there

W

      there's a war on, right?

      there's fallout from wars

      things have to be contained

      'with us or against us'

      am I right?

      listen

      the other guy

      don't let that laconic exterior fool you

G

W   it means he doesn't say much

G   I know what it fucking means

W   alright

      tetchy

      just don't go thinking he's the simple one, ok?

      guy's here for a reason

G   we're all here for a reason

W   ah, no

      he's a bit different, he is

      serious stuff

G   why?

W

      guy's educated

      studied stuff

G

W   look

      you wanted to know what's going on out here, right?

      well

      it's him

      people like him

G

W   ah, forget it

doesn't matter

just, you know
be aware

WOLSTEAD takes a photo.

G

W   I'm going out by the ovens for a bit
      keep warm
G   what do you mean?
      sun's out
W   is it?

      I get cold easy

      you don't get cold?
G   what, here?
      fuck, no
      I'm fucking roasting
W

      you will
      just you wait
G

      thought you said you hadn't seen any ovens
W

      I haven't
G   you haven't?
W   you said they were out the front, right?
      pretty sure I can find them

WOLSTEAD exits.

Alarm sounds.

45

G   jesus
always fucking looking after them
always fucking watering
fucking chinky spic nigger fuckers
eh?
eh?
and you just fucking sit there
bunch of lazycunt fucking sand wogs

there you are
shuffle off this mortal coil, you cunt
it's nothing you wouldn't do to us

christ
I've had enough of this shit

jesus it's so hot

GRAINER *sprays himself with water.*

G   oh
now that's an idea
oh, that's a fucking great idea
ah
god
that's so much better

none for you fuckers now, I'm afraid
oh no
who's going to look after you if I'm not well
eh?
got to look after number one, don't we?

h)

TANC is painting a symbol on some of the plants.

G

    what's that

T

G   what've you got?

T

    paper

G   ah

    right

T

G   something going on?

    new orders, is it?

T   not for you

G   there something you're not telling us?

T

    course there is

    lots of stuff I don't tell you

    doesn't matter, though

    nothing's changed

    just some stuff I've got to do

G

    right

    heh

    look at you

    cool as a fucking cucumber

    there any air con round here?

T

G   fans or anything?

    no?

Alarm sounds.

G   I'll get it

T

what about the last row?

how do they look?

G   dry

what, you're writing down 'dry'?

T

G

orders, eh?

they're a fucker

so

how many of us are there?

T

G   not just the three of us

seen the bunks and stuff

three for every unit, is it?

two on, one off?

T   you can stop all that right now

G

T   it's not going to work

there's stuff you're better

not supposed to know

you haven't looked in any of them, have you?

so you don't know what's in there

G

T there's a war on, right?

  you don't know what's against us

  but it's out there

  behind doors

  safe

G

T you're doing a good job

  don't fuck it up

Alarm sounds.

G is that

  is that right?

T time to feed them

G I just did

T

  did the alarm go?

G yeah

  but

T feed them

G

i)

WOLSTEAD takes photos at intervals.

G   has he got quieter?

W   who?

G   who do you think?

     him

W   he's always quiet

G   yeah but

     I dunno

     seems weird

W   ah

     he's just got a job to do

     preoccupies him

G   oh

     so you know about this, do you?

W   what?

G   all this new stuff going on

W   what?

     what new stuff?

G   oh come on

     don't you fucking play innocent

W   I have no idea what you're talking about, little one

     you're losing it

     cold's getting to you

G   a) fuck off am I losing it

     b) it's not cold

     I'm fucking roasting here

W   stop shouting

G   I'm shouting because I don't like being kept in the dark

     ok?

W   you're not being kept in the dark

     I have no idea what you're talking about

G   you're a fucking liar

W   fine

G

    all the paper

W

    what?

G   all that paper that's arrived

    big fuck-off bundle of the stuff

    all typed out

    new orders or something

    all them charts and tables and whatnot

    tickboxes and stuff

    you must have seen them

W

G   look

    something's happened, alright?

    don't play dumb

W   not playing anything

G   yeah

W   look, alright then

    so something new's turned up

    so what?

    doesn't affect us

G   it might

W   if it did, we'd know about it

G   very trusting all of a sudden, aren't you?

W

    look

    it doesn't matter what it is

    it's not going to change anything

    if he's not telling you anything,

    just means he's got more work to do now, doesn't it?

    leave him to it

    you keep pushing him, you might end up having to do it

    couldn't have that, now could we?

G

     you'd better not be keeping this shit from me

W   or what?

G   just better not

GRAINER is shaking a photo.

W   I've told you it doesn't do anything

     the pictures

G   not doing it for that

     it's a fan

     keeps me cool

W   right

     it doesn't do anything

G   you said

     why do you care?

W

     can't you just fuck off for a bit?

G   where?

     hmm?

     and do what?

     there's nothing to do

W   I don't know

     anything

     christ, you're like a fucking child sometimes

     you could find me a jacket, for a start

G   what?

W   a

     jacket

     a coat, or something

     must be one around somewhere

G   what do you need a jacket for?

     it's roasting

W   piss off it is

```
        look, feel my hands
G       I'm not feeling your fucking hands, ok?
W       jesus
        you're a child
G
```

GRAINER leaves.
WOLSTEAD sits.

Time passes.

TANC enters. He records the plants with a Dictaphone, conducts some strange tests.

TANC leaves.

GRAINER comes back in.

```
G       well?
W
        well what?
G       what happened?
        what did he do?
W
        nothing
```

j)

TANC holds a flame next to one of the plants.
He seems dissatisfied with the results.
He makes some notes.
He does this a few more times.

k)

Incredibly loud music is being played at the plants from a tiny portable stereo positioned close to them.
GRAINER has removed much of his clothing to keep cool.
He sprays himself with water occasionally.
WOLSTEAD has wrapped up warmly.
They both sit.

Time passes.

The music stops.

G

W

G

W

    WHAT?

G   what?

W   WHAT DO YOU WANT?

G   nothing

W   fucking stop staring at me then

    jesus

G   I'm not staring at you

W   don't

    just fucking don't

    alright?

G   jesus

    alright

W

    you using your shirt?

G   what?

W   your shirt

    are you using it?

G   no

W   thank you

    fucking hell

G   don't mention it
W
G

TANC enters, consults a list, puts some of the plants on a tray, and leaves with them.

Alarm sounds.

G   least there's a couple less of them now
W

      give me the spray

      give me the fucking spray

G
W   thank you
G   I need that back
W   yeah yeah
G   you're their favourite
W   shut up
G   you love them
W   shut up
      child

WOLSTEAD takes a photo.

W   thought they didn't like the cold
G   what?
W   that's why they grow in spring
      cos it's warmer
G   it's not cold
W   fuck off
G

      are you serious?
      can you not feel it?
      it's boiling
      I'm cooking over here

W   just stop it, alright?

      fucking mind games

G   I'm not

      oh forget it

W

      I get it

      I know what's going on

      he's put you up to this, hasn't he?

G   who?

W   him

      the

      the first guy

      'Make him think he's always cold then he'll go completely off
      his fucking nut'

      like he isn't already

      they all think I'm fucking insane

G   who 'all'?

      no one's put me up to anything

      jesus

      calm the fuck down

W   I'd be perfectly fucking calm if you'd all stop fucking with my
      head

G   I'm not

      look forget it

W

      so you're saying I'm crazy

      is that it?

G

      look

      maybe there's something wrong

      glands or something

      makes your body think it's too cold

      should go and see someone about it

W   who?

```
      no fucking way
      when's the last time you saw someone else?
      hmm?
G     there's others out there
W     oh, there are, yeah?
      so you and all these other people out there
      you're getting to know each other
      spending a lot of time together?
      so are they all doctors
      or just most of them
      hmm?
G     jesus
      alright
      whatever you want
```

WOLSTEAD takes a photo.
Alarm sounds.
The music restarts.

```
W
      you have any spare socks?
```

l)

TANC's face is very close to one of the plants. He starts caressing, licking and sucking it, his behaviour becoming increasingly sexual, until he's violently chewing the plant as he masturbates.

When he's finished, he spits the plant out.

The neon lights start to fail.
The sun shines brighter.
It begins to snow.

m)

WOLSTEAD is wearing as much clothing as he can find, in front of a crude heater.

GRAINER wears as little as possible while maintaining uniform, surrounded by fans.

G   point that fucking thing away from me

W   what?

G   the heater

point it away

W   it's not pointing at you

G   it fucking is

I can feel the bastard thing

W   it isn't

jesus

happy?

G

I can still feel it

W   you're a tiny, pathetic child

trapped in the body of a FUCKING PRICK

WOLSTEAD take a photo.

W   you look a right picture, you do

literally now, as it happens

G   get fucked

W   you get hypothermia

it's not my fault

you got anything spare?

G   you're wearing all my fucking clothes

TANC enters, and starts taking away all the plants marked with a symbol sprayed on them.

W   you know

I think he has got quieter

G

Alarm sounds.

W

you know what the thing about torture is?
G   what?
W

torture
torturing things
G   what do you mean?
W
G   we're not torturing anyone
W   no
no
sure
G   we're just keeping watch
W   yeah
course

but you
no, hang on
the thing
that's right
you know what the thing is?
G   what?
W   the thing
the thing about torture

thing is
and what no one fucking tells you

it doesn't work
G   no?
W   nope

problem is
the guilty ones tell you fuck all
the innocent ones tell you anything
can't trust anything someone tells you while you're sticking
I don't know
needles in their balls
or whatever

G   four on the five
and you'd know all about this
would you?

W   more than you'd think

G   I see
you've tortured people, have you?

W

I'm just saying
doesn't work

G   yeah it does
course it does

W   I'm telling you

G   I know you're telling me
but you're fucking wrong
because you're cooking your brain

W   it's fucking freezing

G   what about all these attacks, hmm?
these prisoners tell them all about their plans, don't they?
and then we all get fucking saved

W   oh, right
attacks
and how do we know about these attacks, then?

G   just comes out, doesn't it?

W   uh huh
and who do you think lets it come out?

G   oh fuck off

W   no, come on
you're nearly there

G fuck
  off

W we get told by the people doing the torturing
  don't we?
  these attacks that never happen
  of course they got averted by our glorious intelligence
  services, didn't they?
  course they did
  it couldn't be that there was never a single, solitary chance
  that anything was going to fucking happen
  oh no
  the powers that be averted a disaster, through their thorough
  intelligence and resourcefulness
  course they did

  and they've got to be allowed to continue with their work, to
  protect the good and innocent people of the land
  and as long as we're safe
  we don't want to know what's going on to keep it that way,
  do we?

G jesus

W

G so why do they do it, then?
  hmm?
  if it doesn't do anything
  why's it so fucking popular?

W

  don't know
  got to do something, haven't they?

WOLSTEAD takes a photo.

G that fucking camera

  give us a go

W   why?

G   cos you look ridiculous

think mister and missus might like to see how their son's
going off his nut

GRAINER takes a photo.

G

no

no, you're wrong
people are just brutal fuckers
that's all it is

you find someone who's hurt you
and you hurt them
and you keep hurting them

and you make sure their friends know about it
and that your friends know about it
and you keep hurting them

makes you feel better

W   now you're thinking

G   fuck off

point that fucking heater away

The music begins again.

n)

TANC separates the remaining plants into groups.
He stacks one of the groups into a pyramid.
He smashes one of the groups on the floor.

o)

The snow has become increasingly heavy and settled.
The sun has become brighter.
WOLSTEAD is building an igloo.

W   jesus
         where've you been?

G   went that way
         walked for about 40 minutes, I think
         then I turned round and came back again

W

G   there's nothing there
         it just keeps going
         out to the horizon

         the fuck is that?

W   igloo

G   I can see it's an igloo
         what are you building an igloo for?

W   look
         if we're going to have to stay here, then we'll need some
         shelter
         you want to abandon the post, fine
         I'm staying

G   it'll melt

W   it won't melt
         not until it warms up again, at least
         when it won't matter

G   jesus
         you're like
         like when you get a fever or something
         shivering when you're overheating

W   a bit like that, yeah
         except it's about forty below
         so I'm building an igloo so we don't freeze to death

```
        you're welcome
G       fuck's sake
        whatever keeps you busy
        what about them?
W       what about them?
G
W       fuck 'em
        they'll be fine
        things make it through winter all the time
G       seven on the eight
W       I know
G       you've got an ace there
        look
W       I fucking know
        I've a few other things on my mind right now
        alright?
```

Alarm sounds.

```
G
        when were you off last?
W       oh, I don't know
        lost track
        the other guy's never around, anyway
        we've got to stay on it
        national security and such
G
        seriously
        I'm a bit worried about you

W       jesus

        you know
        loads of people die in the mountains
        exposure
        when they get found, loads of them are naked
```

clothes folded up all neat just next to them

when you're getting hypothermic, your heart rate slows
down
blood vessels open up
fwoofh
makes you feel really hot

so these people just strip off in the middle of the snow
and they get even colder

you want to watch out for that
G   I'm fine
will be, anyway
once I get in the shade

you done that before?
W   nope
G   is it going to work?
W

find out, won't we?

p)

TANC pulls a cloth tight over some of the plants.
He slowly pours water over it until it's drenched.
He repeats a few times.
He fills some of the pots until they're overflowing with water.

q)

GRAINER has a scalpel.

G   I'm really
     really not happy with this
W   no
     seriously
     I've been looking into it
     reading
     books and things
     like you said
     might be something wrong, yeah
     not glands, though –
     there's a bit of your brain that controls your temperature
G
W   you want me to die?
     I'm going to freeze to death

     come on, come on, come on

Alarm sounds. They ignore it.

G   you sure about this?
W   fuck's sake
     just do it
G   hang on
     quick picture
     for posterity

GRAINER takes a photo.

G   alright
     ready?
W   hang on
     wait

     alright

```
        hang on, wait, wait
        if something happens
G       if something happens?
W       if
        you can have me camera
        yeah?
G       fucking hell

        yeah, alright
W       alright

        you can't stop
        alright?
G

        alright
W       I'm serious
        ok?
G

W       alright

        come on then
```

GRAINER cuts through WOLSTEAD's eye with the scalpel.

```
G       fuckfuckfuck
        oh jesus

        how is it?
W

        not as bad
        's I thought
G

        feel any better?
```

W

    nm

    come on

GRAINER cuts deeper into WOLSTEAD's eye socket.

G   anything?

W   fuck

    come on

    put your back into it

    I'm freezing to death

G

    this right?

W   yeah

    come on

    get on with it

    come on

GRAINER scrapes around with the scalpel.

W   fuck

    eugh

    oh

    oh god

    's better

G   jesus

W

G

W   missed a bit

G   fuck's sake

W   come on

    again

G   fuck off
         I'm not

GRAINER vomits.

W   fuck's sake

         give it to me

r)

Time passes.

TANC enters.
He takes off his shoes and socks, uproots several of the plants, and pours the soil over his feet.

Time passes.

He makes some notes.

s)

WOLSTEAD, blinded and hypothermic, is curled up in the foetal position.
GRAINER is too weak from the heat to move.
TANC is motionless, rooted in soil.

The sun shines.
They are all becoming buried in snow.

Alarm sounds.

GRAINER murmurs to himself.

G   it's alright

     it's alright

     it's alright

GRAINER drags *WOLSTEAD* over, and arranges him in front of *TANC*.

GRAINER takes a photo and sits at *TANC*'s feet, shaking it.

The snow falls more heavily.
The sun shines more brightly.

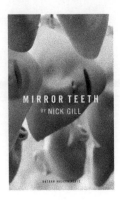